# THIRTY-FIVE GREAT IDEAS

---

## TIMELESS ADVICE FOR FINANCIAL SUCCESS

Andrew M. Hudick, MS, CFP

Fee-Only Financial Planning , LC. Roanoke, VA

ISBN 978-0-9847743-0-2

Printed in the United States of America.

**Ecclesiastes 1:9-10**

What has been will be again,
what has been done will be done again;
there is nothing new under the sun.
Is there anything of which one can say,
"Look! This is something new"?
It was here already, long ago;
it was here before our time.

# CONTENTS

# ACKNOWLEDGMENTS

I was fortunate to have many positive influences on my writing for this project. Anne-Marie Hudick edited many of these articles before they were originally published. While meeting Anne helped me become a better person and therefore a better writer, her impact on me is immeasurable. Anne is always striving for her best and that drive and energy improves those around her. This collection is a direct result of her motivational spirit.

Andrew Michael Hudick III tediously entered the articles from various prior formats into the current format depicted in this book. Margaret Eden Bowen used her talents to put it all together and figured out how to put my suggestions into the shape you see now. Evan Goncalo helped create the vision for the cover of this book, incorporating the vista that inspires us daily.

Versions of many of these articles were previously published in The Blue Ridge Regional Business Journal, the Practical Accountant, and Blue Ridge Business Journal. I hope you enjoy them today if you missed them the first time.

# FOREWORD

I met Andrew Hudick in November 1995. He was incoming President for NAPFA (The National Association of Personal Financial Advisors) host of the conference we were both attending and the trade organization for fee-only financial planners. We bonded in mutual outrage that a vendor, hawking what was proclaimed as rare and previously undiscovered JFK documents as an investment opportunity, was creating interest within our peer group. It was not the last time we were appalled at the next big thing in investing. The JFK documents turned out to be a hoax and some of our peers lost money along with their clients.

It was evident to us we shared a world view not common in financial planning. We agreed cash flow was the cornerstone, without it success was highly dependent upon luck. From Andy I learned "1/3, 1/3, 1/3"- one third of income is earmarked for savings, one third for taxes, one third for spending. We ruthlessly examined the cost of investment first, ahead of perceived merit. We decried debt as investment leverage. We were early proponents that asset allocation was superior to investment wizardry. These and other concepts did not endear us to some of our peers, or even later our colleagues. Thankfully, another trait we shared was fortitude. We married in 1998. We combined our financial planning practices in 2001. Both endure.

The idea for this book germinated from a habit of saving articles to use as teaching tools with clients. Contenders for "the file" were not often found in the top financial press. We privately referred to their headlines of "Earn 12% Risk Free" and "How To Invest Like A Billionaire" as financial porn. The articles in our files were simplistic and generic, timeless in their relevance. Many of them were written by Andy. When our practice included mentoring financial planning interns, this file was required reading. It was their first lesson, and it was an important one. If it was all they ever learned from us, the trials we endured over this phase of our career can be considered worthwhile.

2016 marks thirty-five years since Andrew Hudick began his practice. What follows are thirty-five of his favorite articles since 1981.

Anne Marie Hudick, CFP
November 2016

# PREFACE

A personal Financial Plan is a dynamic set of ideas. Your life and the decisions you make are ongoing. Having structure with your finances will allow you the best chance to accomplish the goals you set out for yourself.

There is a lot written or broadcast on the topic of personal finance and presented as news. Over my thirty-five years of practice as a comprehensive fee-only financial advisor, I have encountered very little that is new. Whether I am called upon to write an article or a financial plan, my strength has been in keeping it simple. The idea for this book was that personal finance is often depicted as complex or even intimidating. Maybe some of my articles published over the years would bring clarity to someone and create the motivation needed for success.

We ordered the articles in the same order I would approach a financial plan. We included each article's original publication date. We resisted edits, so tax rates and interest percentages are reflective of publication date rather than current conditions. The underlying concepts stand.

There were a few omissions in our archives. As technology has advanced, I hadn't written on computer hacking or cyber scams. Also, with more of our clients segueing into retirement communities, I wanted to address this transition. Article 35, Scams and You, and

Article 31, Living Large at the End, are published for the first time in this book.

You might wonder why there is nothing included about college planning. This is intentional. Unlike the other ideas presented, education funding is not an absolute for families. Parents should prioritize their own retirement planning and debt elimination ahead of funding a child's education. In my experience, young adults thrive using a variety of approaches to higher education that are not readily foreseen. If you can accomplish the things put forth in this book then you will, perforce, have the capacity to participate in your child's life decisions.

Thank you for giving my words consideration. I hope you find them effective to accomplishing your own goals.

Andrew M. Hudick II
November 2016

# 1

## FINANCIAL PLANNING: THE MORE IT CHANGES...

### SEPTEMBER 2006

Five years ago we had a new planner join our office and one of the file folders we had her review included the cache of one page periodical clippings I had accumulated. This folder contained ideas and techniques of financial planning options and each was written and reported in a succinct manner. It is a skill to write and report. It is a greater skill to do so concisely and the authors of these articles had mastered that skill.

As our new planner reviewed the file she commented on the dates of the articles. Many of the bylines were from the 1980's. One of the beautiful things about the financial world is that there are a lot of absolutes. The tools and techniques you use to create an integrated financial plan have not changed a lot over the years.

In a recent issue of the BRBJ, General Manager Tom Field in his column, "The Crow's Nest", relayed how his nine year old daughter skipped through his recent column of well thought out filler and helped him reduce the entire column to a sentence. As his daughter correctly pointed out, keeping it simple is an art. As Tom held forth in his column, he is still learning.

In this same BRBJ issue, Editor Dan Smith in his column, "In My Opinion", wrote about getting old and leading the edge of the boomer generation and his amazing discovery that not all that much has changed in his lifetime. Many things were still the same for him as they were for his parents. While it took Dan several column inches to make this point, he got there in his own way. Even though many things in the world change, the basic principles stay the same.

We had another new planner join our firm this year and last month the planner who has been here five years gave the new planner the one page clippings folder. I heard him speaking to her about the articles and discussing the dates of some of the articles. She was explaining that many of the concepts have not changed over the years and that much of what we do is to help people simplify their finances and state things in a more concise manner.

We are a mobile and connected society. We are stressed and informed on a variety of levels. We have full work days and full weekend schedules. We have beepers and pagers and huckleberries and cell phones. We have e-mail and facsimile machines. We have passwords and personal identification numbers and four-digit codes and six-digit codes. We have different codes for the office and the home burglary alarms. We have codes that require numbers and letters. We have different codes to access our personal and business accounts. When we get confused, we call an 800 number and have to explain our dilemma to someone located in India...oh wait, that is another column.

So, there you have it. Not a lot changes so if it is new and exciting but it cannot be explained in a few sentences it is likely not a good financial planning idea. A good idea can be explained succinctly and the best ideas from yesterday are still being used today.

By the way, our new planner has taken the clippings folder and scanned those old pages into our computer. We now have an electronic cache of the old brown paper articles saved on a disk and accessible through the computer system in our building. Maybe there is room for a few new good ideas...now if someone could just explain to me how to find my articles on the electronic archive list!

# 2

---

## NEW SHOES

### JUNE 1990

I have been wearing the wrong size shoes for much of my adult life. Wrong length. Wrong width.

A consumer of habit, I did not know that I was buying the wrong size shoe. I simply continued buying the same size shoe year after year without allowing for any change or growth in my feet.

The other day I stopped in a shoe store. Not the shoe department in a men's clothing store, nor the shoe section in a department store, nor a discount shoe store. A "real" shoe store with a shoe salesman who measured my feet. Prior to our meeting, my closest relationship with a shoe salesperson had been to watch Al Bundy on "Married with Children."

My salesman watched as I selected the style of shoe I wanted, a black loafer (the same style I always select—I probably should change this too), and then asked me if he could measure my feet. As he did so, he asked what size I normally wear and informed me that he would bring two sizes of the loafer for me to try, the size I normally wear and the size he thinks I should wear. I would simply select the style that was more comfortable.

After I selected the size suggested by my salesman, he told me that many people he saw were wearing the wrong size shoe. Seeing no reason to have their feet measured, they continue to buy the same incorrectly sized shoes throughout their lives. As uninformed consumers, we simply adapt to what we have and make it work.

Most of us have semi-annual dental check-ups, thanks to promotions by the American Dental Association. Many of us have periodic physicals, thanks to promotions by the American Medical Association. Few of us, however, follow through with having our feet measured on a periodic basis. We just do not think about the changes our feet undergo.

The same is true of our personal finances. There are a very large number of people who own the wrong kind and amount of life insurance, are paying taxes on too much income (and therefore paying too many taxes), do not have an up-to-date estate plan, or have inefficient and inadequate investments. These people simply need to have a periodic check-up. The decisions being made today are based on old data using old ideas and outdated products. If you do not know about the changes that have occurred, you simply adapt what you have and make it work. Look for improvements.

As our lives change, so do our needs. Look at the many new and varied financial products that have been developed in the last several years. It is easy to see why the old ways of computing taxable income, buying an investment, selecting an insurance policy, or planning your future are no longer accurate.

Many consumers waste a large portion of their income through a combination of outdated ideas and products. What used to work well in years past may not necessarily be the best method today. Take some time and review your financial situation. Become better informed. Attend a class or subscribe to a contemporary magazine.

In addition to improving your health with semi-annual dental check-ups, annual physicals, and bi-annual shoe fittings – add a periodic financial review and improve your wealth.

# 3

## NO PLAN, NO ACTION

### AUGUST 2011

My Editor sent me a request for my simplified version of what I have learned about investing after closing in on thirty years of being a fee-only financial planner. "In a nutshell" he called it.

Make a plan; take the action. It sounds so simple when you write it down. It is not so simple in practice. Make a plan, take the actions required to complete the plan.

I have met with thousands of people over the years and heard their stories and seen the results of their efforts and actions. The successful people and families have a purpose, a goal, and a system and they implement the actions to make the system function. The unsuccessful folks have similar goals but do not have a workable system or fail to actually make the system work.

I have seen folks be successful with their investment goals by buying real estate, by buying stocks, and by buying bonds. Each form of investment has had various good and bad years but the secret to being successful in accumulating the financial resources needed to reach the goal for themselves and their family was to create a system; and then to implement the system.

There is no magic answer or magic formula. You just need a little diligence in working the plan. You first need a plan and to have the plan you need a goal and then with the purpose defined you can create the set of steps you need to take to make the action a reality.

Are you a good parent? Are you good at a sport? Are you more than competent at your chosen career? None of this happened without you creating some version of a plan and working toward achieving a result you found acceptable. So it is in investing.

Write down your goals for your investments. Create a system that will allow you to be successful. Follow the system.

This seems so basic but after thirty years of watching individual investors and their families succeed and/or fail this is what it comes down to... create a plan. Then follow it.

# 4

## FINANCIAL PLANNING HAS A BROAD MEANING

### MARCH 1993

*Your financial plan covers a lot of ground and it's up to you to know what that ground consists of.*

Financial planning has become a catch-all term in most consumer finance journals. While the meaning of "financial planning" is fairly well defined, the term is used to reference many related concepts and even as a marketing tool for certain disciplines. There is no legal or regulatory threshold that must be met to call yourself a financial planner.

One version of the generally accepted definition of financial planning includes the following: an integrated approach to coordinate the cash flow, insurance, tax, investment, retirement, and estate needs of an individual or family.

To prepare a financial review or a financial "plan," goals should be clearly defined and each aspect of an individual's finances should be reviewed to make certain they are consistent with the established goals. You cannot make an investment decision without considering the tax ramifications and you should not make an insurance decision without knowing your cash flow and investment positions.

In most consumer finance journals, a journalist will use the term "financial planning" when she is writing an article about "investment planning," "tax planning," "insurance planning" or "estate planning." The article could be as mundane or unhelpful as picking the "top five mutual funds to buy now" and it will be titled as a financial planning article and the people quoted as experts will be called financial planners.

## Ignorance and Bliss

Most of the journalists who write these articles are new to their careers as writers and are therefore relatively young. They do not have a financial planner themselves nor do they have a financial plan in place that they are following.

They are writing about a concept they do not understand completely because they have never experienced it personally and often they are being taught the concept by those they are interviewing. While the sign of a good journalist is to report and write about an event or a concept and explain the topic so the reader can understand there is often a disconnect in some of these articles. If the journalist is using an expert who has a financial interest in the subject being reviewed, she should reveal this fact to the reader.

When you include the fact that many insurance and investment professionals use the term "financial planner" to describe their roles, the confusion to the consumer often increases.

Many sales professionals use the term "financial planner" "financial consultant" or "financial advisor" to describe their career. Since the use of the term planner/consultant/advisor implies that advice is being offered, the consumer has a right to expect that this advice not be one-dimensional. If your financial advisor is really an insurance or investment salesman, he should tell you this.

## Misinformation

There is a lot of misinformation offered with regard to personal finances. Some of this misinformation results from misleading comments, uninformed opinions, and distorted facts. One of the things that could be improved is the correct use of terminology by the media and by those who work in the various financial planning disciplines.

Do not make the mistake of confusing someone who has expertise in insurance planning, tax planning, estate planning or investment planning as someone who is an expert in financial planning.

You should also make certain that anyone who calls himself a financial planner is not holding himself out to be an expert in some other discipline if he is not. There is no guarantee of truth in advertising in this industry.

# 5

---

## ON SAVING MONEY

### OCTOBER 1989

Ask your neighbors and co-workers what their most difficult financial task is and the over-whelming response will be "saving money." This simple fact has prevented many families from accomplishing their specific financial goals on time.

If you cannot set aside funds in a systematic and periodic fashion, you cannot save for retirement, your child's education, your 25th wedding anniversary, your vacation and you may not even be able to save enough until the next payday.

Since proper and efficient management of your cash flow is the cornerstone to successful accomplishment of the majority of your financial goals, here are some ideas to help you set those funds aside.

1. If you have money in your checkbook, do you feel "rich" and therefore able to spend? If so, segregate your savings by placing it into another account.

2. Do you run up credit cards to their limit, use your savings to pay them off, and then repeat the process?

If so, consider reducing your credit card limit, eliminating some of the cards you carry (the average consumer has eight credit cards), or leave the cards at home.

3. If you are married and one of you is designated as the billpayer, that person should also be the saver. A joint effort must be made so that the non-billpaying spouse is not using the "savings" to make consumer purchases.

4. The easiest way for many to save is through a payroll deduction account. This can include placing funds into a credit union, buying savings bonds, or using an employer-sponsored thrift plan (such as TSA, IRA or 401(k) plan.)

5. A similar approach can be used by having a periodic amount deducted from your checking account and placed into a stock, bond, or money market mutual fund.

6. One of the tried and true methods includes "pay yourself first," which forces you to set aside the savings first and allows you to spend the balance of the paycheck. Many people pay their bills and end the month with little, if anything, for themselves. If you don't know where to start, you probably won't. The place to start is at the top.

7. An easy way to start your savings plan is with a bonus or by saving your annual raise and continuing to live on the previous salary amount.

8. Try reducing the number of times you eat meals away from home and save the difference. Or, if you travel

and use personal funds for business expense and are later reimbursed for this item, place the reimbursement check into savings.

Capturing and saving funds on a periodic basis can be accomplished, but you need to determine a method of saving that will work for you. Since you will use your savings to start your investment program to help you accomplish your major financial goals, this one activity is the foundation to help you meet your financial plans.

# 6

---

## PREPARING YOUR STATEMENT

### SEPTEMBER 1992

When was the last time you prepared a financial statement? Often referred to as a balance sheet, this is a listing of your assets, your liabilities, and your net worth. When prepared correctly, your statement of financial position is a valuable planning tool. This "snapshot" of your finances is a beginning point in preparing a financial review and a good way to look at your financial life in a holistic manner.

Many financial mistakes are made by individuals who do not look at the big picture. They view their investments, their mortgage, and their retirement plan as separate things. In order to become more successful in your financial dealings, you need to consider each financial decision as an integrated part of your whole financial situation.

For instance, many people have accumulated a nice savings account. They also carry credit card balances from month to month. With bank savings accounts paying 3 - 4 percent and credit card balances accruing at 12 - 21 percent, why finance consumer purchases? It is more logical to simply pay these consumer debts off.

Other people nearing retirement age or who have retired are concerned about the types of fixed-income investments they should own to help supplement their pension during retirement. This type of investment may pay taxable income in the 7 - 8 percent range. Yet these folks are still carrying home mortgages in the 8 - 9 percent range. They are paying the interest on their home mortgage in order to gain "a tax deduction" and many are losing money on this exchange.

Many Blue Ridge region employees have an opportunity to participate in employer-sponsored savings accounts. These accounts offer the opportunity to purchase a variety of investments including company stock. If you take advantage of this program (and you should) and buy predominately company stock, what happens if your industry suffers a setback? Not only is your current financial position threatened due to a possible job layoff, but your future financial position is threatened as your company stock declines in value. If you look at your finances in a holistic manner, diversification away from the industry that provides your livelihood is prudent.

You also need to look at your entire investment portfolio as one program. Your IRA, your company-sponsored 401(k), your college education fund, and your savings account are all interrelated parts of your investment picture. In order to have a balanced investment portfolio, you cannot make decisions for each account independent of the other. In many cases, one or more of the investment programs offer you an opportunity to purchase either debt or equity investments at a discount. This option should be incorporated into your financial review.

Constructing a financial statement is a good way to start viewing your financial plan in a more holistic manner. By integrating your decisions you can maximize your tax and investment returns while minimizing your transaction costs.

# 7

## FACING FIXED INCOME

### AUGUST 1991

If your salary has been frozen and you are unlikely to earn either a pay raise or a bonus this year, a careful review of your expenses is mandatory. With inflation increasing at a six to seven percent rate over last year, you are actually losing ground this year if you cannot reduce your expenses.

When dealing with a fixed income amount, a careful review of your fixed expenses is often the only way to improve your cash flow. While the ideas offered in this article should be reviewed by everyone, they are especially valuable to those with little hope of a pay increase.

For many, the payment of insurance premiums represents the third largest annual expense item (after taxes and housing). A careful review of the value received for the premium paid often results in a more efficient purchase.

Often, both spouses have family health insurance policies that offer duplicative coverage. Many people will even buy "supplemental" health insurance products that are unnecessary since the coverage offered simply repeats those health benefits already owned. Many times, policies that are sold as catastrophic care, cancer protection, dread disease coverage, or accidental death are so limited in their scope that the premium dollars could be better used elsewhere. Buying a good major medical policy that covers "all" diseases and accidents is less expensive than to buy a variety of individual policies that offer limited protection.

While you are reviewing your insurance policies, take time to read over your home and auto policies as well. Many people can reduce the annual cost by removing unnecessary riders or raising deductibles. If you are a member of an auto club you may not need the towing and labor rider. Or if you have life and disability insurance under a separate individual policy, you do not need to repeat these forms of coverage on your auto policy. You should also meet with your property and casualty agent and investigate whether raising the deductibles would help to reduce the cost. And, you should ask your agent whether you can take advantage of a discount package by placing your home and auto policies with the same insurance company.

If you are making mortgage payments, you should also check your escrow statement. If you were unable to invest at least 20 percent of your original home purchase price as a down payment, you likely were required to purchase private mortgage insurance. This premium, typically $20 to $40 per month, will continue to be paid by you until the equity in your home reaches the 20 percent level. It is, however, up to you to determine whether this insurance is no longer required. Review your escrow statement and then speak with your mortgage company to find out the procedure to have this coverage removed.

And finally, you need to analyze your cash flow and place yourself and your family on a budget or a reduced spending plan. Review your daily living expenses and see which items are really necessary or can be reduced. Once unnecessary expenses are identified, take steps to begin reducing them. This is the most difficult task you will perform. When your income is rising, it is easy to add "fixed" expenses - it is not so easy to begin reducing these same expense items when your income is frozen or reduced.

# 8

---

## TAKE TIME TO UNDERSTAND
## COMPANY BENEFITS

### SEPTEMBER 2003

When was the last time you looked at your employee benefits handbook? Can you find this booklet or set of brochures? Have you ever actually read your employee benefits handbook? Do you understand your employee benefits?

Most people, when accepting new employment, are inundated with forms to fill out and file and often never find the time to actually understand the benefits they have signed up to receive. If you have not taken the time to review your benefits booklet, plan to do so. The benefits provided represent a significant cost to your employer and a concurrent value to you. In many cases, the benefits provided to you as an employee can represent as much as 20-25 percent of your total compensation package. At a minimum, most employers provide several thousand dollars in annual benefits to each employee.

When developing a financial plan or performing a financial review, you want to make certain you take full advantage of the benefits provided by your employer. Duplicating these benefits or leaving gaps in the coverage provided by your employer is inefficient and could generate financial problems.

Most employee benefits take the form of insurance and retirement products. Before you venture out and purchase supplemental products, make certain you understand what is provided to you by your employer. Group life, disability and health benefits often are provided to employees and an opportunity to purchase supplemental coverage (at reduced group prices) is also available. Many people have some form of coverage in place when starting with a new employer or purchase supplemental individual products that duplicate the benefits provided by their employer. Make certain you have coordinated your policies in an efficient manner. You also should remember that many products priced for individual purchase are more expensive than the reduced group pricing option.

When buying insurance, "buy a lot for a little." Purchase large limits of coverage with high deductibles in order to reduce your premium cost and reduce your risk in case of catastrophe. Low deductible and "first dollar" coverage insurance is expensive and often unnecessary.

In addition, be careful about purchasing specific disease supplemental coverage that seems inexpensive. Often, this form of coverage is actually quite costly when measured against the probability of receiving any benefits.

If your employer provides a retirement plan, use it. If this is a matching plan, make certain you contribute your own monies in order to receive the match from the employer. If your employer provides the matching contribution to you in company stock, accept those shares but do not buy additional shares of your company stock. If your company offers a defined benefit plan, you might be wise to consider this option as the "fixed income" portion of your retirement plan asset allocation model. Supplement this investment sector with a growth option using your personal funds. Do not duplicate the benefits the company provides, supplement them.

If your company offers a cash balance plan, integrate the options you choose through this plan with your outside investments. You want to be certain the company monies and your outside investments provide you with the best chance to meet personal retirement goals.

You need to be conversant with the benefits provided to you by your company. Since the benefits package is a significant part of your compensation structure, you should make these options work for you. Take time this week to find your copy of the benefits booklet(s) and make certain you understand what you are paying to own.

# 9

---

## BUY A LOT OF INSURANCE FOR A LITTLE MONEY

### APRIL 2008

*It's a good time to think about − and look into − your insurance coverage because it is vital to your financial health.*

If you survived the 70 mile-an-hour winds we experienced a few weeks ago, you should be grateful. Many of your neighbors were not so fortunate. With signs and trees and barns blown over coupled with the loss of power in many neighborhoods, there was a lot of inconvenience, not to mention the financial expense associated with repairs and cleanup.

As you observed the smoke from the fires and the trees leaning against houses and vehicles, did you consider your own situation? Did you think about the financial protections you have in place? Do you have a working relationship with your property and casualty agent? Have you reviewed the coverage you have in place recently to make certain you have no gaps or overlaps in your limits of protection?

A typical homeowners insurance policy should cover the cost to repair or rebuild your residence. Does your policy do this for you? If the wind blew your roof shingles into the yard or knocked your tree onto your home, would you be protected? A quick telephone call to your agent is a good way to start this investigation.

What if your tree is blown onto your neighbor's home or your neighbor's garage and vehicle? Does your homeowner's policy offer sufficient coverage to protect you against this liability to someone else or his or her property?

What if your vehicle was the cause of a several-car pile-up and you were operating the vehicle? Do you have sufficient coverage to protect you and anyone else who may have been injured? Good liability limits are important and relatively inexpensive.

Everyone is required to have an automobile insurance policy and every homeowner or tenant should have an insurance policy to protect himself and his home. Not everyone with a policy has adequate protection.

## Umbrella

Ask your property and casualty agent about the advisability of adding an umbrella liability policy as part of your coverage. This policy is generally inexpensive (around $150 a year) considering the protection offered (typically $1,000,000). Buying a lot for a little is an oft-repeated saying in the insurance industry.

While you are speaking with your agent to upgrade your level of protection, ask him to also look at the various deductibles you are paying on your home and automobile. It is likely that you are paying more to insure and replace your vehicle (a relatively low value asset for most of us) than you are to insure your dwelling (an asset with a much higher value than your vehicle). If you are trying to budget your insurance premium dollars, work with your agent to make certain you are paying logical amounts for coverage limits.

Remember that the primary purpose of buying insurance is to cover a risk that you cannot afford. You can afford to repair a dented bumper. You cannot afford to replace someone's income for life if you severely injure her in an auto accident. You can afford to replace your television if your home is struck by lightning and it fries your new HD TV. You probably cannot afford to replace your home if it burns down.

Ask your agent to work through your three property and casualty policies for you (home, auto and umbrella) looking for gaps or overlaps in coverage. Ask to see if you have guaranteed replacement cost coverage on your dwelling. Ask for different deductibles to see how this affects the total premium you will be charged.

Make an informed choice on your level of protection and the price you pay for the coverage. This recent windstorm is another reminder that we cannot control everything around us. Use this weather event as the reason to become better acquainted with your property and casualty agent and put together an insurance program that will offer you good liability and property coverage. Buy a lot for a little.

# 10

---

## DISABILITY – CRUCIAL INSURANCE

### JULY 1990

Disability insurance is probably the most significant omission in our personal safety net. You own health insurance. You own life insurance. You have insured your home and auto. But you have yet to insure your earning power.

The greatest single asset we possess is the ability to generate income on a daily and annual basis. If this ability were interrupted due to an accident or sickness, where would the money to fund family living expenses come from?

The easy and logical answer is from a disability income policy. Unfortunately, the majority of the business and professional people reading this article are underinsured. Too many professionals investigated the purchase of a disability income policy, but did not make the purchase because of "premium shock." Traditional policies carry a high annual premium.

There is some good news from the marketing departments of the major insurance companies. They have heard the complaints regarding contracts and have developed a premium scale that is 20 to 50 percent lower than their normal premiums.

The policy, known as an annually renewable disability income policy or ARDI, is the disability income policy equivalent to term life insurance.

In fact, ARDI works much like term life insurance. The standard disability income policy has a fixed premium that stays the same as long as you remain insured (much like a whole life contract.) With ARDI, the premiums start low and increase slightly every year.

The real advantage of an ARDI contract is that you can purchase a top of the line guaranteed renewable, non-cancellable policy that insures you for your specific occupation at a greatly reduced cost. You also retain the option to convert the policy in a future year to the higher-level premium contract should you need to do so.

With ARDI, you can afford the premium on an amount of coverage that is sufficient to meet your needs during the years that you need coverage. For workers aged 25 to 45 who have dependents, this form of protection is almost mandatory. Your inability to provide income for your family would invite tragedy. (Note: even if you have disability protection as an employee perquisite, it is likely inadequate.)

Until recently, your only option was to buy a level premium product. With ARDI, you have a chance to buy a more affordable product. So, break out the disability income file again and call your agent.

Ask him for quotes from several competing companies, as the rates will vary. Be certain you have a contract that is not cancellable by the company, guaranteed renewable to you as long as you pay the premium, offers partial benefits if you can earn a portion of your income, would pay benefits until age 65, and covers you for the duties of your "own" occupation.

# 11

---

## YOUR MONEY: A BASIC UNDERSTANDING OF HOW WE INVEST

### JUNE 2003

Making an investment decision is often an emotional and frustrating experience. Several university research departments have published their findings as to why we invest as we do. This new knowledge into how we make investment decisions comes to us from the field of neuroscience. Research scientists have used technology to help try and understand how we invest.

One of their findings is that the human brain is really good at recognizing short-term trends or making emotional decisions quickly. Our brains are not designed to recognize long-term trends or to compare and contrast a variety of information. Most of the findings are based on the fact that we evolved as hunter-gatherers and our brain adapted to dealing with the things we needed to do in order to stay alive. Finding food, shelter, or a mate did not require our brain to evolve to a very high level.

Our brain makes decisions based on fear. Our brain makes decisions based on past patterns. Our brain makes decisions based on our feelings. Our brain tells us to take a risk to obtain a big reward. None of these reactions will help to make us better investors. These findings reinforce the notion that we make many decisions based on fear and greed.

How can we use this newest research by the neuroscientists to aid us? Some of the old investment adages remain valid even with these new findings. In order to remove fear and greed, set up an automatic investment program. Each paycheck or every month, send in the same amount to be invested. If this occurs automatically, you will continue making your investment even when your emotions may be telling you to stop.

In order to remove the chance that you will try and predict the future, set up a diversified investment plan. Having an investment plan and following a diversified and planned approach to allocating your monies can reduce the volatility of your holdings. A portfolio that maintains a well-diversified mix of stocks, bonds, and cash has proven statistically to maintain a modest risk tolerance for an investor.

In order to remove the risk that you will try to obtain a big reward, you will need a commitment to utilize this investment plan to make future investment decisions. Asset allocation, the method of allotting a percentage of your investment dollars to a specific asset class such as stocks, bonds, or cash, is a useful tool in constructing an investment plan designed to deliver an investment return over time.

An asset allocation program also provides a framework within which to make buying and selling decisions. If your program was designed to hold 50 percent in stocks and now holds 40 percent in stocks, buy more stocks until your allocation returns to the 50 percent level. The neuroscientists have proven that some of the old rules of investing remain valid. Set up a system and application program for your investment purchases that is simple to follow.

Diversify your investments across a broad range of assets. By having systems for purchasing, diversifying and allocating your assets that are easy to remember, you should be able to remove the fear, greed, and prognostication problems that your brain has been trained to offer.

# 12

---

## MONEY AND TIME

### MAY 1990

We are all familiar with the adage "time is money." Most of us relate this saying to the cost of buying services. We know that two hours of work will cost twice as much as one hour. We don't, however, take this "time is money" concept and relate it to our own investments.

Usually referred to as "time value of money," most investments state their anticipated or realized rate of return using the "time is money" concept. This concept is easily understood by using bank certificates of deposit as an example. The nominal rate is stated as 8.25 percent with this total being paid to you on a daily basis as simple interest. You could, however, earn a compounded yield of 8.5 percent if you left your funds in the account rather than withdrawing them as they were earned.

As you can see, the "time value of money" theory works in your favor the longer you leave your money invested. It is a simple concept, but one that is not used by a majority of investors. The area most overlooked is with our retirement plans.

Tax season is the time many of us determine the amount of our eligible contribution to our personal retirement plans. The time value of money idea works equally well for IRAs, SEP-IRAs, 401(k)s, 403(b)s or pension and profit-sharing plans. The rule is the same. In order to earn the maximum return, we should not be making our 1989 tax year contribution in 1990. Instead, we should be making our 1990 annual contribution as early in 1990 as possible.

For instance, if you made your retirement plan contribution in January of the current year, rather than in April of the following year, your compounded rate of return would be much higher. Making a $2,000 annual investment for 10 years with a 10 percent rate of return would grow to $35,000 with a current year January contribution date versus a total return of $29,000 with a contribution date of April of the following year. The difference is only 15 months in time, but the value is more than 20 percent greater.

Again, time can work either for or against you as you plan for retirement. Compare the 19-year old who invests $2,000 a year from ages 19 through 25 and never makes another contribution, with a 25-year old who makes a $2,000 contribution each year from ages 25 through 65. The 19-year old's total investment is $14,000 over seven years and this money remains invested until he is age 65. The 25-year old has a total investment of $80,000 over 40 years. Who has the most money at retirement age?

Procrastination is an expensive habit. The 19-year-old would have a higher total with his $14,000 investment than the 25-year-old would with his $80,000 total. The time value of money concept really works.

You should start your retirement plan saving as soon as possible. Put your full retirement plan contribution in this month. If you save early, you may not have to save as often.

# 13

## WHAT DO YOU THINK YOU KNOW?

### November 2008

*A little advice for the skittish investor. Understand the markets. Be patient. Diversify.*

For the past few months the financial markets have experienced huge price swings with some assets declining in price by large amounts in one day only to increase in value by a similar amount the next day. It is hard not to get caught up in current events. This difficulty is compounded by media outlets constantly offering speculation, rumor, and their version of the "facts."

As you watch a financial reporter offer some financial facts and opinions, have you ever wondered whether the reporter actually had any skin in the game? Do these folks have equity investments? Do they own bonds? Are they investors offering investment advice or just financial reporters creating a buzz? I have often suspected many of them have few investments and one prominent talking head privately says that she has all of her money in one asset class: bonds.

Several months ago oil prices were very high and many news reporters were offering negative comments about the profits being made by oil companies. It was suggested that this was a bad result and somehow these companies were wrong to be making a profit. Congress was talking about "capping profits."

Note what happened to many financial institutions in the past few months as they stopped making profits. Our economy needs our public companies to make a profit. Absent a profit, these companies will not be in business. As we have discovered recently, if these companies are not in business, the effect on you and me can be profound. The profits, or lack of profits, impact each of us in our pension plans, other investments and even our daily lives.

If you are a speculator, then you should have enjoyed the past few months of activity. If you are a long-term investor then you need to focus on the real world that lies beneath the flow of data and the noise being created. A long-term investor should remember a few of the more challenging moments in the past 25 years:

- The high tax rates of the early 1980s;

- Creation of tax shelters that inflated real estate prices and the subsequent collapse (and government bailout) of the savings and loans in the early 1990s;

- The high-flying stock market fueled by the Internet and dot.com companies that imploded in early 2000;

- And most recently, the "easy credit" available to those with no ability to pay that has helped create our current financial challenge.

The emotions of the moment can distract us if we do not have a plan. It is impossible to predict how markets will move at any time due (in part) to the frenzy created by those feeding us information that prey on our emotions of fear and greed.

If you have a diversified portfolio and some patience, then stay focused on your goals, invest for the long-term, and diversify away some of the risk. Do not concentrate your investments in any one stock, industry, piece of real property, or sector.

My own money is invested in our local real estate, our local industries and the broad stock and bond markets. I am experiencing some of the same discomfort you are, but I have a financial plan. I expect the current challenge to end and the financial system to survive and the talking heads to keep talking. Consider the source before you take action. Markets ebb and flow. We need to have patience and the flow will return.

# 14

## FIGURING THE REAL RATE OF INVESTMENT RETURN

### JULY 2007

Many people have a mistaken notion of the rate of return earned from the price appreciation of a specific investment asset. Others may see someone making a large sum of money from the sale of an asset and do not recognize the work or risk that went into the process to make that money. Still others may make an investment decision without knowing all the rules or laws that would allow them to make a better decision.

I have a friend who told me last week how much money he has made on the price appreciation of his home. He retired and sold his two-story home a little more than six years ago and purchased a one-level patio home.

The home he purchased is in a neighborhood of similar homes (some with garages on the left side of the dwelling unit and some with garages on the right-hand side) and his is beige (as opposed to gray or white). This type of home is in high demand due to the fact that many of you aging boomers have bad knees and backs and want no yard work or extra climbing in your life.

His home value (based on the fact that the similar dwelling unit next to him just sold) has increased nearly 60 percent in the past six years. This 60 percent return is a compounded rate of return of more than eight percent a year (less than the US Equity markets in the same time period) and is certainly a good return. However, it may not be as great a rate of return as it appears.

Remember that the seller of this home is going to pay some transaction fees in order to close the sale of his home and this may include a realtor commission (typically six percent) and some legal and transfer fees (as much as another one percent).

In addition, the owner of the home has been paying around one percent a year of the assessed value of the home in real estate tax. The combination of the charges in six years may be as much or more than 10 percent of the sale price. This will reduce the 60 percent gain to 50 percent and the compounded rate of return will be closer to seven percent than eight percent.

This is still a nice gain but maybe not the rate of return implied by my friend when he said his neighbor was going to make 60 percent on the sale of his home.

Another friend, who works in the real estate industry, has several stories about folks who see the various television shows about fixing up and "flipping" homes for a large profit and think they can do the same thing.

They do not realize that many of the people who do this on television lose money or that the ones who make money have their own sub-contractors or do most of the work themselves. There is quite a risk involved in this process, not to mention the cost of your time and materials. If this enterprise were readily profitable, more real estate professionals would engage in it themselves.

I am reminded of another friend (a member of the Codger Generation) who married late in life and kept his bachelor pad and converted it into a rental unit. He bought a new and larger home with his new wonderful bride.

He soon found out how difficult it is to be a landlord and upon the sale of the rental home he was taxed on the gain. Had he simply sold the bachelor pad when he and his wife purchased the marital dwelling he would have owed no tax on the profit made. Gains made on the sale of a principal residence are tax-free while a gain on the sale of rental real estate is a taxable transaction.

While this fellow still made a profit, he converted part of his gain into a capital gains tax and reduced his total return greatly.

As a used car salesman I know likes to say, "It is not the deal they got, it is the deal they think they got" that makes the transaction a positive event. Dealing in real estate can be profitable but remember that the total return earned may not be as great as it seems to be on the surface.

# 15

## KEEP YOUR HEAD AND STABILIZE YOUR MONEY

### OCTOBER 2007

KISS (Keep It Simple Stupid) is still the best approach to just about everything, including protecting your investments.

If you have experienced concern in the past few weeks over your financial situation, you are not alone. If you did not panic and make a major change as a reaction to a news report or market gyrations, your panic has now passed and your financial situation has stabilized.

You can now choose to make a more rational decision in an attempt to prevent a repeat of your concern over your personal financial situation. If you have read this column over the years, you know that we are big believers in keeping things simple.

If a financial technique or investment theory cannot be explained in a simple and concise manner, we advise against utilizing it. If a financial decision is made out of fear, guilt, greed or ignorance, it should be avoided. Remember that the investment and insurance world is a logical one.

The risks and returns are generally easily defined and measurable. If the idea or opportunity cannot be explained using simple words and concepts, it is unlikely a good option for you. Some financial products are sold using emotion. Some products are marketed using greed or fear.

None of this is new.

The details of the events occurring over the past few weeks may be different, but we have seen similar events before. The financial markets give each of us an opportunity to capture our share of wealth from capitalism. We are able to achieve success by having an investment strategy that includes objectivity and logic.

This process can be streamlined and simplified to remove emotion and make the decisions concrete and efficient. When major financial changes enter the picture, it will have little effect on your individual wealth since you will have a system in place to protect yourself.

**Old ideas**

We think it is a good time to revisit a few ideas covered in past columns that can contribute to your future success. If you already implemented all of these ideas you experienced little concern the past few weeks while the investment markets caused headlines.

- Do not mix your insurance with your investments.

- If you need insurance, buy insurance.

- Do not buy an insurance product that includes an investment component. The cost is high and the result often is poor.

- Buy bonds and put them in your retirement plan. This tactic offers you stability and as close to a guarantee as you can get for tax-deferred compounding and growth.

- Buy stocks and own them outside your retirement plan. This approach allows you to take advantage of the current reduced income tax rate on capital gains and qualified dividends.

- Use a re-balancing program that allows you to add your new money to your losing market sector or sell your winning sectors.

- Do not extend a home mortgage for more than 15 years or a car payment for more than three years.

- If you cannot afford the payment level on a 15-year fixed rate mortgage you are likely buying too much house for your budget.

- If you need a five or seven-year payment term to buy your vehicle, you cannot afford that model. Do not ever lease your vehicle.

- Create a systematic savings program that is integrated with the ideas mentioned above that equals 15 percent to 20 percent of your income. The monies should be invested using your personal investment model and dovetail with your house and car payment program.

- Keep your financial decisions simple.

- Keep them systematized.

- Live within your means.

- Save for the future.

These past few weeks the people who got in trouble bet their mortgage on interest rates staying low. Five years ago, the people who got in trouble bet on technology stocks continuing to rise.

In a future year, you may see people get in trouble who bet that international stocks will continue to grow at double-digit rates. Remember that the details of the past few weeks may be different, but we have seen similar disruptions before. And we will again. Plan ahead and you will not have to be a part of any future panic and concern.

# 16

---

## BE CONSISTENT IN YOUR INVESTMENTS

### DECEMBER 1991

Many professionals, having become successful in their chosen occupations, fail in their investment program and do not achieve the financial goals they seek. While they spend years trying to master their trade and countless hours trying to improve their professional skills, they devote little or no time to investment planning.

Rather than develop a logical and efficient investment program, most people own a disparate collection of investments. This assortment of assets often includes securities held for years that may have once been acquired for a specific reason and then simply forgotten.

Many people have several checking and savings accounts at different institutions, certificates of deposit that are automatically reinvested without a review of rates or maturity dates, and securities that passed to them as gifts or from an inheritance. Most of these assets have not been updated in years.

When a plan, including specific goals and quantified objectives, is not formulated and followed, the investment results will be mediocre. Without an investment objective, savings will simply stagnate and generate a below market return. Rather than investing with a consistent and easily monitored system, many people invest based upon the latest "story" and try to make a large return in a short time. The results are almost always disappointing. In order to be successful with your investments, you need to develop a strategy. Then you need to follow it faithfully. Decide ahead of time the types of investments you are comfortable owning and then make the purchases religiously. There will be times when it will be difficult, but following this one rule is certain to work to your benefit over the years.

Do not allow yourself to be swayed by "experts" who continually suggest that you move into and out of the different investment markets based on changes in economic conditions, interest rates, inflation, or the stock market. Following this advice and making constant changes in your investments almost always results in poor performance.

As you decide on the types of investments to include in your portfolio, remember that the most important rule is diversification. Without adequate diversification, the most well thought out choices can become liabilities, rather than assets.

While the best way for most investors to achieve an adequately diversified portfolio is by owning a series of mutual funds, a diversified individual portfolio can be constructed if you are willing to devote more time and energy.

The greatest annual return most of us will achieve comes from the wage we make practicing our trade. An investment program properly constructed will help you achieve financial independence.

# 17

## CONSIDER GROWTH PORTFOLIO

### FEBRUARY 1992

Would you rather purchase and own government-insured investments, high-yield investments, or high-growth investments? Be honest with yourself. Where do you tend to make investments when you have additional funds for investment? Where are your 401(k) or IRA monies invested?

Think about this: inflation has averaged 6.31 percent over the past 20 years. In 1990, the rate of inflation was 6.11 percent. Please be assured that even though we are experiencing some form of recession, inflation will exist in 1992. Prices of living expenses, including consumer goods and health care, will rise because salaries and other expenses in many industries will continue to increase.

If, in 1990, you owned a government-insured investment, such as a U.S. Treasury obligation or a certificate of deposit (CD), what was your true after-tax rate of return? During 1990, you could purchase a CD from local institutions in the Blue Ridge Region that paid interest in the seven percent to nine percent range. If you were astute enough to buy a nine percent CD, what was your real rate of return?

Most taxpayers in Virginia pay a combined federal and state tax levy of around 33 percent. If you had earned a nine percent return on your certificate of deposit and then paid your tax assessment, your true after-tax rate of return would have been six percent. In 1990, with inflation slightly above six percent, you would not have gained ground with your nine percent investment and you would have been a loser with an eight percent CD.

Government-insured investments are in the four to five percent range today. This four to five percent rate is below the 20-year average rate of inflation. How many of us are still buying Treasury securities and CDs as the major components of our investment mix?

It is easy to discount inflation during our high earning years, when our salaries are increasing at or near the rate of inflation. As consumers, we are accustomed to inflation and simply factor it out of our investment plans. We expect prices to rise and simply discount the importance of this since we also expect our income to rise.

Do not be shortsighted. If inflation averages six percent for the next 20 years, your $1 in purchasing power will drop to 31 cents in value. In other words, in 20 years, it would take $3.21 to purchase what $1 would purchase today.

While this fact must be understood by a retired individual, a wage earner must be aware as well. While retirees know the value of reinvesting a portion of their interest and capital appreciation, those looking forward to retirement must also take inflation into account.

While high growth investments can experience tremendous volatility, their historical long-term trend is up. Indeed, in any 20-year period you choose since 1925, a buy-and-hold investment in stocks has outpaced inflation every time. If you have nightmares because of the volatility of the stock market, start dreaming about the effects of continued increases in inflation. With the results that inflation offers, you must consider making an investment to counteract these increases.

This column is not a blanket endorsement to put all of your funds in high-growth investments (i.e., stocks). It is simply an attempt to make you aware that you are losing a portion of your investment if you are not considering growth in your portfolio.

# 18

---

## KEY TO RECOVERY – TRUST AND FAITH

### MARCH 2009

*What exactly is money, anyway? It's both more and less than you might imagine.*

Our monetary system is based on trust. The difference in purchasing power and value between a $1 bill and a $10 bill is because you and I believe there is a difference. Take a $1 bill out of your pocket and read the words "Federal Reserve Note" and "The United States of America certifies this note is legal tender for all debts, public and private."

Choose another denomination and you will see that the only difference in the paper notes are the suggested values ($1, $5, $10) and the pictures depicted. The manufacturing cost to create each of the paper notes is the same but the implied value differs. There is no asset behind this $1 bill other than the full Faith and Credit of the United States Government. For this value to be real, we have to trust and believe in this statement as fact.

Many of us pay our bills and expenses by check or with a set of online keystrokes. "Real" money is never involved. We send our monetary payment by mail with our signature attached to a check. We send our payment by e-mail with a tracking number attached. Our signature is simply a promise to pay the agreed upon amount. The exchange is one based on trust between honorable people.

The world financial markets operate in a similar way. They operate best when there is trust and transparency. When the parties to financial transactions are honest with one another, business moves along. Commerce and trade occurs between willing buyers and sellers with full disclosure and a sense of trust. If we lose the faith and trust in those that manage financial dealings, we have little left in the financial world. Those dots and dashes and dollar bills do not represent anything that is tangible.

Did your financial vendor put an asset in your investment account with a funny name? Did you own an asset that was full of abbreviations? Did you have an investment that could not be explained simply in a couple of sentences? Did you own an asset that imposed a liquidation penalty that was not based on the current market price of the security?

Have you read about the CEO of the bank or brokerage institution who earned or paid out millions of dollars of bonuses based on the sale of financial products that had no economic viability? Did you read about a former chairman of the NASD and NASDAQ Stock Market who may have bilked his friends and business associates out of $50 billion? Have you read about the proposed cabinet members who neglected to include all of their earned income on their personal tax returns and did not pay their "fair" share? These were financial leaders that we trusted and had faith in assisting us with our financial decisions.

The system failed because a few abused the trust and faith vested in them by the many. This abuse is not an isolated fact pattern. The system has failed before and once the "change" occurs and things start running smoothly again, the system will inevitably fail again. Your job, as a consumer of financial products and services, is to be aware of the options available and to make good decisions with good assistance.

Our financial economy is too complicated to ever return to trading with beads, wampum, or even gold coins. While the system is a manufactured one, it requires faith and trust in order to function. In order for the confidence in the system to return, we each need to do our part. I want to believe in the honor of our leaders and they need me to believe in them in order to serve me most effectively.

I am ready to have my faith in the system restored. Are you?

# 19

## DEFERRING TAXES

### AUGUST 1990

Paying income taxes is an optional event. We have the ability to control the amount of tax we pay by modifying our taxable income.

Tax deferral and tax elimination methods along with a variety of tax deductions and tax exemptions provide available options. In our quest to reduce the amount of tax we pay, many of us have turned to income tax deferral methods offered through life insurance products and annuities.

Tax deferral would always be beneficial if there was no cost associated with this process. Since life insurance products and annuities have administrative expenses and other costs that lower the advertised yield, the advantage of tax deferral offered through these products is not as great as it would appear. In fact, an investor can lose money through such a deferral contract and careful analysis is required before investing.

Many insurance and annuity products sold today have significant administrative costs associated with them. Yield reductions of two to three percent are quite common. While the quoted rates are often comparable to, or greater than, the rates being offered on investments, the "net" result is often a return that is less than advertised.

In fact, many sales presentations include the comparison to a CD investment. Nothing could be more misleading. A standard certificate of deposit issued through a banking institution presents you with a "net" yield. With a CD, the overhead and administrative expenses are removed before computing the rate of return. With many annuities, the guaranteed "rate" is often computed before figuring the overhead costs. Once the administrative expenses are deducted from the guarantee rate, the advertised return from an annuity or insurance product is greatly reduced.

Even with this somewhat misleading advertising, buying a tax-deferred annuity product or single premium life insurance product can be advantageous. This is true even though the net return in this type of product is often less than the net return offered by similar investments that are not tax-deferred.

Earning a lower rate of return in a tax-deferred investment will always give a higher overall return than earning a higher return in an after-tax investment if you can wait long enough.

With time on your side, even fighting the high overhead costs of these products, a tax-deferred investment can be worthwhile. Assuming a combined tax bracket of 35 percent, we find that an eight percent tax-deferred return would surpass a nine percent taxable return in 13 years. If we increase the difference between the two investments to two percent, we find a 24-year breakeven point.

If we reduce the return of our comparable investments, the time required to break even increases. That is, at a seven percent deferred rate and an eight percent taxable rate, we would need to maintain the investment for 16 years. Increasing the difference in yield will simply add time to the breakeven requirement.

Taxpayers in a low tax bracket or with short time horizons on their investment holdings will be less likely to profit from this type of deferral. Since annuities and investment life insurance are often sold to retirees or as a retirement supplement, a careful analysis is required.

Please note: the advertised return offered by many annuities and insurance products is not the true return. You need to read carefully to find this number. If one of your goals is beating the tax collector, examine several methods to find the one most beneficial for you. Each situation is different.

# 20

---

## TAKE SOME TIME TO REVIEW YOUR TAX FORM

### JUNE 2008

*A little investigative work on what this financial outline says about you could result in a bonus for you.*

At the risk of sounding boring (this is, after all, a financial planning column), have you reviewed your most recent Form 1040 now that some time has passed since you filed it? Have you pulled out your personal income tax return and looked at it now that the rush to file in a timely manner has passed?

If you had another person prepare the return, it is highly likely you did not even look at the return other than to "sign here" when you picked up your packet at the preparer's office. Bad move. There is a wealth of information included in your income tax return and much of this information can be used by you to plan your financial future.

Want to create an investment plan? Before doing this, you would always look at your income tax return to see what you earn and how you earn it.

Trying to decide what type of retirement plan to use and what form of income to use to fund it? Before doing this, you would always look at your income tax return to see what you earn and how you earn it.

Trying to decide on an amount of life insurance or disability insurance? Before making this final decision, you would need to know what your income level is and how the money is being earned.

Planning to make some changes to your estate plan? Yep, your income tax return has a direct bearing on these decisions as well.

Why not take a few minutes this week and read your personal Form 1040 U.S. Personal Income Tax Return? While we have written columns in the past on the deductions available to you, we want you to concentrate today on the "income" portion of the return. On the Form 1040 these are lines 7 thru 22.

Do you have entries in this section on different lines? Do you have wages, dividends, interest, business earnings, capital gains, rental receipts? Each line item carries with it a planning opportunity. Now is the time to think about these planning opportunities.

If you used a CPA or individual tax preparer, consider calling the preparer to see if she can meet with you to review your return. Let her know it is a planning or exploratory meeting. If she cannot assist you, ask for a referral.

Your goal is to use your income tax return to plan for next year. The first question you will ask is, "If I could have done things differently last year and earned the same amount of money, how could I have paid less income tax?" If you are like most people, you will have several choices of things you can consider doing for next year (which, by the way, is now halfway over). Your goal from the meeting is to see if there is a way to turn some of the tax you paid into savings for your future.

I suspect that if you invest an hour in this process, you will find ways to save a sum equal to several days of your regular wage. Then the only decision for you will be whether you wish to take advantage of the opportunities you discovered. The process is likely to be less boring than it sounds.

# 21

## SOCIAL SECURITY: A TAX

### SEPTEMBER 1989

Look at your last pay stub and notice the amount of Social Security tax being withheld. If you earn $48,000 this year, you will pay $3,605 as an employee and $6,250 if you are self-employed. In addition, if you are an employee, your company pays a matching tax of $3,605.

The money paid into the Social Security system is often referred to as a contribution. You do not contribute; you are taxed. The Social Security Administration is willing to report your personal earnings history and a summary of your estimated benefits. You probably assume that your Social Security contributions are being credited to your individual account and that when you retire, you are guaranteed that you can begin drawing against your account balance. That is not the case.

Social Security is a tax, not an entitlement. There is no guarantee that when you retire the Social Security system will provide for you in the same way it is providing for today's retirees. There is no certainty that your Social Security contributions will guarantee you a middle-income standard of retirement living.

A person who retired at 65 in 1988, after paying the maximum Social Security rate over a 45-year period, would have paid cumulative Social Security taxes of $38,000. This person's monthly benefit check would be approximately $838. (The maximum benefit for a 1989 retiree is $899 per month.) At the rate of $838, 45 years of contributions would be paid back in less than four years. At 65, a person has a life expectancy of 16 to 20 years and could receive many times the contribution amount in benefits.

Compare this to a worker who entered the work world at age 22 in 1980 and who pays the maximum tax through a 43-year career. If the worker retires in 2023 at 65, it is estimated that the equivalent of $475,000 in Social Security taxes would have been paid. With an estimated benefit of $1,250 per month, it would take this person until age 97 to recoup the "investment" into the Social Security system. In addition, since this worker was born after 1938, full benefits cannot be applied for before he is 66 years, 8 months old.

During the late 1940s, the contributions of 13 working people supported each Social Security recipient. Today there are 3.4 workers and by 2010 there will be two workers to support each recipient.

As the number of retirees continues to increase, the benefits being paid are increasing. With Social Security tax rates at 7.51 percent for an employee (with a matching 7.51 percent for the employer) and 13.02 percent for self-employed individuals, today's workers are making substantial contributions to keep this system solvent and support today's retirees.

Many forecasters do not expect the current system to remain in place. Some form of a "needs" test will likely be developed in order for today's worker to qualify for a monthly income at retirement. Many methods have been proposed and while it is impossible to predict what method of needs testing will be chosen, it is likely that many of us will be "too wealthy" to qualify under the accepted proposal. Social Security benefits will likely only be available to those at low levels of income and net worth.

Studies have shown that many Americans view their Social Security contributions as a substitute for retirement savings. We need to stop thinking of Social Security as an entitlement and guaranteed retirement program and acknowledge it for what it is: a tax. It is not a savings plan. We need to begin saving for retirement in other ways.

If you are considering retirement and are younger than 50, you would be wise not to include the Social Security system as either a primary or secondary source of income for your retirement. Be certain you have provided for yourself with other forms of savings and invested in a supplemental retirement account.

# 22

## FEAR, EMBEZZLEMENT AND FIDUCIARIES

### JULY 2009

*If you're having second thoughts about financial advice in general and your advisor in particular, here's how to protect yourself and your money.*

Are you fearful that your investment account is unprotected and that your money could be embezzled? Do you think that your financial advisor could be involved in a Ponzi scheme? Do you worry that your savings and investments are at risk from something other than market fluctuations?

Every week there seems to be another report about a financial advisor accused of manipulating investment accounts for the advisor's (and not the customer's) gain. I am amazed at some of the things that consumers have allowed to happen with their money and the results the actions produced. There is a simple strategy that you can use to protect your money.

If you have hired someone to assist you in making investment decisions, be certain this person (or entity) does not maintain custody of the funds that they are managing. You want a large, solid financial entity holding custody of your assets. Examples of this type of entity would be Fidelity, Vanguard, Schwab, TD Ameritrade, or Merrill Lynch.

The custodian of your assets should not be the person giving the advice. Keep the advisor and the custodian separate. Do not write a deposit check for your account payable to the individual name of your advisor; send the deposit check to the advisor payable in the name of the institutional custodian.

Nearly every story of theft or embezzlement of funds involves an individual who is serving as both the advisor and the custodian of the account. If you separate the functions, you minimize your risk. Your large institutional custodial entity has a set of rules in place that prohibit their customer's monies from being moved by the advisor outside of the customer's account. These rules are set up for everyone's benefit. Your custodian will generate an independent periodic written report and allow you to view your financial assets on a secure Web site. Your custodian has a duty to protect your assets from theft.

There is also a duty that your advisor should have to you. Your adviser should be regulated by the Securities and Exchange Commission (SEC). An SEC-registered advisor pledges to act out of a "fiduciary duty" and is obligated to put their clients' interests before their own. You need to understand this key fact. If you have a stockbroker as an advisor, you may not have someone who is putting your interests first.

There is an important distinction between a stockbroker who is regulated by the Financial Industry Regulatory Authority (FINRA) and an SEC-registered investment adviser. A broker can recommend any product that is "suitable" for a customer. A broker can sell you any investment that they have reasonable grounds for believing is suitable for you. An SEC-registered advisor is required by law to have a higher standard of care for their client than a FINRA-registered broker.

The conflict of interest that exists in the financial planning world is real so make certain you are aware of the rules that govern your relationship with your money. In order to have the highest degree of safety in your financial dealings, your money should be held separately from your SEC-registered financial advisor.

# 23

---

## EVERYONE NEEDS A WILL

### FEBRUARY 1987

Many folks fail to appreciate the full importance of a will. They may think their asset total is too small or too simple to justify the time and expense of preparing a final document. Even if you think you have sufficient assets and recognize the need for a will you may not have one. This could be due to procrastination or a subconscious refusal to accept your own mortality.

Here are five basic reasons for having a will:

### Reason 1: To Choose Beneficiaries

If you do not have a valid Will, the intestate succession laws of your state of residence will determine how your property is distributed after your death. For example, most of the property of an unmarried, childless decedent who dies intestate (i.e., without a will) generally will be distributed to his or her parents (or siblings if there are no parents). The property of a married person with children who dies intestate may be distributed one-third to the spouse and two-thirds to the children. These distributions may be contrary to your personal wishes. By failing to prepare a Will, you allow the state to select your beneficiaries. A Will allows you to determine not only who will receive the property, but also how much each beneficiary will receive.

## Reason 2: To Control Taxes

With the changing rules for taxation of assets and the current large limits allowed before taxes are levied, many feel they do not need a will because they do not have a taxable estate. However, an estate is often larger than anticipated because of resources that are often overlooked because they are illiquid or forgotten. Some examples include life insurance policies, qualified retirement plan benefits, or IRAs. These forgotten resources can be left outside of your Will to your chosen beneficiary or a charity. All assets should be considered when writing your will so you can coordinate the distribution of your entire estate. A will, properly prepared, can reduce or remove the taxation for many estates.

## Reason 3: To Appoint a Guardian

A will can be used to name a guardian for your minor children in the event of the death of you and your spouse. If you are a single parent, you will want to choose a guardian for your children rather than forcing the state to select one for you. While naming a guardian does not always bind the named guardian or the court, it does indicate your wishes and most courts generally will accept your direction.

## Reason 4: To Name an Executor

Without a will, you cannot choose someone you trust to carry out the administration of your estate. If you do not specifically name an executor in your will, the court will appoint an administrator to handle the estate. There is an advantage in selecting as executor someone who knows your situation and can follow your wishes.

## Reason 5: To Establish Domicile

You may wish to establish your domicile in a particular state for income tax filing purposes or other reasons. If you move frequently or have homes in more than one state, each state in which you reside for part of the year could claim you were a resident of that state at the time of your death. This could subject your estate to multiple probate proceedings and overlapping claims to state death or inheritance taxes. To minimize the risk of this multiple taxation you should execute a will that clearly indicates your intended state of domicile.

# 24

---

## GETTING THE MOST FROM A TRUST

### NOVEMBER 1991

For many, using a trust as part of your estate planning is logical. Trusts accomplish two things: tax savings and control. If you have life insurance, a residence and a retirement plan, you can easily have an estate tax problem. The typical fee for preparing a trust document (several hundred dollars) can easily be repaid to your family in taxes saved.

The control motive involves protecting heirs from themselves and others. Immature heirs with money and too much freedom can easily lose the funds. A scheming friend or relative can help dispose of an inheritance in an inappropriate fashion. And, funds left in a well-worded trust can be kept away from creditors and bankruptcy claims. In any case, you trade the cost of the trust for peace of mind.

If you are a candidate for a trust, the most important thing you can do is to carefully select the trustee. The best trust can be destroyed by a poor trustee.

Trusts are legal beings, and if you create one, you are putting assets into an entity governed by state law. Trusts are managed by trustees who invest and pay out the assets on behalf of beneficiaries according to the terms of the trust, the law and their own discretion.

A trustee can be either an individual or a corporation. There are pros and cons to each choice. An individual trustee, such as a family member, a friend or advisor, may have a good understanding of your wishes. They can also minimize or reduce fees and will also likely be more flexible in working with the heirs to achieve your wishes.

On the other hand, a corporate trustee will not die. They are not managing trusts in their spare time and they might have access to good record-keeping services along with good tax and investment advice. A corporate trustee is more expensive and often more bureaucratic. The beneficiaries of the trust may have to deal with many different representatives since a corporate trustee often experiences high employee turnover.

While fraud is more likely with an individual trustee, mismanagement can be found in both individual and corporate trustees. And, quality varies greatly. Since a corporation is made up of individuals, before hiring a corporate trustee, pay them a visit. Meet the individuals who will be handling your trust and ask about their background and experience. Also take your heirs to get their opinion. After all, if the trust is activated, you will not be here and the trustee and the heirs will be working together.

With your legal advisor's help, you may want to consider using both an individual and a corporate trustee, delegating duties to the strengths of each. You will also need to consider removal and succession of trustees. Give someone the power to change trustees if they perform poorly. Make certain you have named an alternate to an individual trustee and be certain you are clear on the annual costs involved to administer the trust.

Including a trust document in your estate plan can offer both control over your assets and tax savings. Investigating the possible advantages in your situation could be quite beneficial.

# 25

---

## USING WILLS, TRUSTS

### MARCH 1993

Like most people, you have probably accumulated more possessions than you ever expected. The total value of your home, retirement accounts, and life insurance benefits is likely to be fairly substantial. It is therefore important to think about who will inherit your wealth when you are no longer around to enjoy these physical assets.

You can designate ownership of your assets in four basic ways by:

- Writing a will:

- establishing a trust;

- leaving assets by contract; or

- allowing the Commonwealth of Virginia to decide distribution for you.

Using a will or a trust allows you to control who will receive your assets. Also, if your documents are properly prepared, you can accomplish a variety of other benefits, including a reduction of estate taxes, leaving specific bequests to individuals or charities, naming a guardian for your (minor) children, or arranging for a manager or successor to your business.

Leaving assets under a contract arrangement can typically bypass trusts and will documents. Contract assets include beneficiary designations under life insurance contracts, annuity contracts, and retirement plan contracts. Other examples of assets that will pass by contract are jointly titled properties such as savings accounts, real estate, and investment accounts.

While the contract method of asset distribution may help you to accomplish some of your inheritance goals, it can also create certain problems. Indeed, since a contract transfer takes place immediately upon death, if the will or trust is not the beneficiary or joint-owner, these assets pass outside of the will or trust arrangement. It is imperative that you review the beneficiary under your contract arrangements as your distribution wishes change.

As unbelievable as it may sound, over one-half of all adult Americans allow their states' laws to determine who inherits their assets (this is known as "dying intestate"). In Virginia, this could mean that your spouse inherits only one-third of your assets while your children split the remaining two-thirds.

Proper coordination in your estate planning is the key. Use of a will in conjunction with a trust can generally save your estate a variety of taxes and administrative expenses. In addition, if you coordinate certain contract assets with these documents, you can provide a variety of contingencies. While the investment (of both time and money) to prepare the proper documentation may seem high, the cost of incomplete preparation after a death or disability occurs can be truly overwhelming.

# 26

---

## BACKUP SYSTEMS

### SEPTEMBER 1990

While many small business owners have "backup systems" in place for their technology and some even have a backup system as a management technique, how many of us have put in place a backup system to manage our personal affairs?

With the chances of becoming disabled being much greater than the chance of dying during most of our lives, having a backup system in place to plan for disability is essential.

Planning for the possibility of disability usually includes the design of an income replacement insurance program, the purchase of a good major medical hospitalization program, and even the consideration of long-term care coverage. Each of these options is costly as it entails the payment of an annual premium.

Many of us overlook another inexpensive, yet vital, disability planning device. It is simple, but very effective. It is the durable power of attorney. As a backup system for personal or business planning, it has no equal.

An ordinary power of attorney is a document in which the principal authorizes another person, the attorney-in-fact, to act in his stead. The power can be limited to specific acts, such as granting the attorney-in-fact authority to pay bills. Or the power can be quite broad, authorizing the attorney-in-fact to engage in any act that the principal could normally perform.

The biggest problem with an ordinary power of attorney is that it becomes worthless if you become incompetent. If you become mentally incapacitated and unable to handle your affairs, a regular power of attorney automatically terminates. Since a period of disability is when the power of attorney is most useful, you need to be certain your document is a "durable" power of attorney.

By definition, a "durable" power of attorney is a power of attorney that is not terminated by subsequent disability or incapacity of the principal. A durable power of attorney, along with a will, is an integral part of nearly every financial plan.

Once put in force, a durable power of attorney will normally not terminate until the death of the principal. (Of course, while competent, a principal can always revoke the power of attorney.) It is therefore extremely important who you choose as your attorney-in-fact. Often spouses name one another as their attorneys-in-fact.

Many times you may want to consider another mature and responsible person, such as your adult child, to handle your affairs. And, you should consider naming an alternate attorney-in-fact in case your chosen representative is unable to serve or is unavailable when needed.

A business owner may consider executing two separate durable powers of attorney: one for his business and one for his personal affairs. While a spouse may be the appropriate choice for the personal and family matters, another individual may be a better selection as the attorney-in-fact for the business.

Everyone is equally at risk when it comes to losing their mental abilities and therefore being a candidate for a durable power of attorney. There are, however, several alternatives when deciding the best way to handle your durable power of attorney. As with any type of legal document, you should consult with your legal advisor prior to executing this part of your backup system.

# 27

---

## BEWARE LIVING TRUSTS

### MARCH 1991

The revocable living trust can be an appropriate estate-planning tool when used properly. However, many estate planners claim that the living trust solves all estate planning problems. Always better than a will and certainly better than jointly owned property, they say. Don't believe it!

When you obtain your financial and estate planning advice from folks who have one service or product to sell, it should not surprise you that the recommendation you receive includes the purchase of their product or use of their service. It therefore follows that the people who most often recommend living trusts are the same people who sell books on the topic or who call themselves living trust specialists.

In 1965, Norman Dacey published the book, How to Avoid Probate. It was full of dire warnings of the costs, dangers, delays and scandals associated with probating a will. His book spawned a host of people offering the living trust as the best way to avoid probate. Recently, some of these trust peddlers have again surfaced. They offer free living trust seminars or to send free living trust information, and then suggest that the living trust is for everyone.

The living trust is not a new concept (as they would have you believe) nor does not having a living trust subject you to supposed astronomical costs associated with probating.

The primary reason cited for setting up a revocable living trust is that property placed in trust does not go through probate. Avoidance of probate allegedly saves time upon your death and allows your property to pass quickly and easily to the people you have chosen to inherit it.

The probate process was designed to ensure that a deceased person's will is certified valid by a court and that the person's property is distributed to its rightful inheritors. The quicker and more efficiently the distribution of assets can be handled, the better.

While an efficient transfer of assets is certainly a goal of many of us, in many cases this goal can be accomplished using a properly-drawn will. The probate process has been simplified since 1965 and many estates are efficiently handled and settled quickly without the use of a trust. High costs, delays, and problems within the probate process are the exception rather than the rule.

The proponents of living trusts claim that having a trust saves money by reducing the costs of probate, protects your privacy, and removes the chance for claims against the estate. In some cases, this is true; but not in every case.

For many, having a will is the best solution. For others, a will and a power of attorney solves these problems. And, for some, titling certain property jointly in conjunction with a will and power of attorney would be the best solution. All of these options are less expensive to set up than a trust. So, while a trust is appropriate in many situations, it does not solve all estate planning problems.

Do not be swayed by those who sell the "loving" trust as the only way to care for your dependents and beneficiaries. While living trusts work well for some, and can distribute assets to loved ones in an efficient manner, it is not the panacea some prominent advocates claim. As with many financial decisions, there are no cure-all solutions available. Estate planning is no different.

# 28

---

## TOO LATE TO START? IT'S NEVER TOO LATE

### OCTOBER 2004

*Ok, so you've been too busy living to bite into this retirement stuff. You can still get started and the earlier you move, the better off you'll be.*

Are you worried about being successful in your retirement planning attempt because you are getting a late start saving and investing?

For many, raising children, changing careers, divorce or just plain living have delayed their attempts to save and invest as they wish they had in previous years.

For those with the woulda, shoulda, coulda blues, don't give up. The same investment rules apply to late starters as to those with retirement ambitions who started saving earlier in life. Buy a diverse mix of stocks and bonds and try to do so when possible in a tax-deferred investment such as an IRA, 401(k), 403 (b) or similar plan.

While there is no substitute for due diligence and diversification and use of the time value-of-money concept, if you are a late starter, this article is for you.

Many financial advisors and most financial magazine authors who write on the topic of total income needed during retirement suggest that you need to replace 70 to 90 percent of your working income in order to enjoy a comfortable retirement.

While many of us may want to replace 70 to 90 percent of our earned income during our retired years, we do not necessarily need to. We would suggest that for most of us, about 50 percent of our current income is used to support our lifestyle. The other 50 percent is being used for taxes, debt service (i.e. interest) and funding our savings for our future retirement.

Take some time and work through where you actually spend your money. Start with your 2003 income tax return and note how many tax dollars you paid. You paid more than five percent toward Virginia income tax, more than seven percent toward FICA, and more than 20 percent toward Federal income tax.

Add in your mortgage interest listed on Schedule A and it is likely you spent about 40 percent of your total income you claimed for 2003 for something other than normal living expenses. If you save even a modest 10 percent of your earnings, you have accounted for 50 percent of your total revenue being used for something other than living expenses.

The suggestion here is not to be discouraged because you procrastinated. You should start saving now in the company 401(k) or set up a Roth or regular IRA and put the maximum annually ($3,500 in 2004) into that account.

Start saving now, as your goal is a fairly modest and attainable one. You should also consider setting up your home mortgage to be paid off when you retire. This fixed payment need not be a part of your retirement obligation.

There are a variety of articles, including worksheets, thoughts and assumptions at a web site found at www.early-retirement.org. The ideas represented on those pages should give any retirement procrastinators confidence in the future.

# 29

## FACING LONG-TERM CARE

### FEBRUARY 1991

The fastest-growing segment of our population today consists of those aged 65 and older. With medical advances allowing Americans to live longer (the average unisex life expectancy is now 88), many individuals are rightfully concerned about the costs involved with long-term care.

Of those reaching and exceeding the age of 85, nearly half will fall victim to Alzheimer's disease. This disease, and other forms of chronic illness and disability, may well require large amounts of capital that cannot be met with traditional health care insurance policies.

In fact, Medicare only pays for an average of two percent of all long-term care costs. In addition, most private health plans, including major medical coverage, provide little or no protection against increasing long-term care costs. The national average for a stay in a nursing home is 30 months and, in Virginia, the average monthly cost of a private pay nursing home is $2,180. It is easy to see that the cost of an extended long-term care stay can become quite expensive.

Many of us could face the prospect of having nursing home care greatly reduce the financial resources we have spent our lifetime accumulating. Because of this potential expense, the decision to buy a long-term care insurance policy has become an important financial planning issue. Long-term care insurance is designed, like many insurance products, to protect your assets. Your need for this form of insurance protection varies with the amount of your assets.

You do not need this coverage if you do not have assets to protect. For those of modest means, the cost of insurance will likely be prohibitive and your financial resources can be better spent on normal daily living expenses. Since Medicaid will pay for nursing home coverage, many people who enter a nursing home will simply spend down their assets to become eligible for Medicaid payments.

You also do not need this coverage if you have a large asset total. If you can generate an income level (from investments or your pension) that will greatly exceed the cost of nursing home monthly fees, your financial resources will be relatively unaffected by the cost of paying for nursing home care. If you can self-fund, a long-term care insurance policy is not a necessity for you.

Those who really need long-term care coverage fall in the middle. If you have accumulated a good net worth with an adequate monthly income but cannot afford to generate funds for both your spouse's household expenses and your own nursing home stay, you should consider a long-term care policy. In your case, if you require nursing home care, you need the supplemental income a policy of this type would generate.

Often, a good time to buy coverage is when you are nearing retirement and discontinuing your disability income policy. The premiums will be similar and, as your earned income decreases, your ability to meet increased health care costs is reduced. When comparing policies from different companies, do not rely on the marketing materials from the company for a complete explanation of coverage limits. Request a copy of the actual policy and review it carefully. Review each section of the document with your agent until you understand it fully.

Each long-term care policy contains several restrictions and limitations. Collect as much information as you can before making a purchase. Do not let fear or other emotions control this decision. Remember, not everyone will require long-term care and for those that do, some combination of personal resources and public services is a viable option.

# 30

## INVESTMENT ADVICE: PRESERVING YOUR LIFESTYLE IN RETIREMENT

### JUNE 2003

Retirement is one of life's major adjustments. While many of us simply think, "Will I have sufficient financial wealth to fund my retirement?" the decision to retire is more involved and includes lifestyle issues as well as financial options.

When to retire is a very personal decision that must be reviewed carefully. The following list of questions should help you assess your own retirement position. As you weigh the pros and cons of retirement, you will find that some of the answers to these questions are fairly obvious, others more subtle.

How much is my monthly retirement check? What percentage of my normal salary does this represent? Do I have the option to draw a supplement from my other retirement savings (IRA, 403(b), 401(k), etc.)? Should I adjust my household budget? Does my pension payment include some form of cost-of-living adjustment? How will I cope with the fact that inflation will erode the purchasing power of my retirement check?

At a 5 percent inflation rate, one dollar will only be worth 61 cents in ten years. Even a 2 percent inflation rate will reduce one dollar to 82 cents in 10 years. How do I plan to adjust for this increased cost of living?

How will I obtain health insurance? What is the expected cost? Upon obtaining the age of Medicare coverage, will my policy coordinate with Medicare adequately? What options do I have? Does my insurance cover home health care? If I need to move to a nursing home, what will this cost be and can I expect some help from my current insurance program?

Is my current home my retirement home? Should I consider a retirement community, a smaller home, a different part of the country? Can I afford the upkeep and real estate taxes of my current home during retirement?

Am I emotionally ready to retire? Have I developed outside interests, hobbies, or volunteer activities that do not relate to my current job or profession? How will I spend my time if it does not involve my daily commutes and the time I spend between those trips?

If you have determined the answers to these questions, you have a great chance of enjoying a successful retirement. If not, now is the time to start thinking about some of these questions.

Most financial retirement concerns can be resolved if your savings plan during your working years is adequate. A good rule of thumb is to save 15% of your salary and invest it in a disciplined manner. The use of an IRA or company sponsored savings plan (401(k), 403(b)) is the most efficient method.

Most retirees need a fairly healthy savings plan in order to be able to draw a supplemental income check to improve their pension or social security payments. Many people postpone or procrastinate in dealing with these retirement planning decisions, especially the idea of setting aside a certain sum of money periodically. You should begin this process as soon (or as late) as the minute you realize the importance and necessity of the task.

The earlier you start the planning process, the greater the depth and range of options (and therefore benefits) available to you. Do not despair if the years have passed more quickly than you realized. If you have accomplished little toward securing your retirement, find answers to the questions posed above and combine them with the other ideas presented in this supplemental section and get started.

# 31

---

## LIVING LARGE AT THE END

### JULY 2016

When someone says they are moving to a "nursing home" what do you think of? Does a covered porch with rocking and wheel chairs come to mind? Do you envision a bunch of folks with canes and walkers wandering the halls? Do you think of double rooms with hospital beds and screens between the beds and little or no privacy, with cafeteria food delivered on trays?

Today the nursing home community bears little resemblance to what our grandparents knew. Many are comprised of retirees who pursue active lifestyles while enjoying on site fine dining and a host of various amenities.

If you have not visited a "level of care" community, you should do so. Many facilities are self-contained with up to four levels of care. You move in while you are ambulatory (a requirement in most places) and able to care for yourself in most ways. As your health fails you have options for different levels of assistance and skilled nursing. Many communities offer memory care services, with an Alzheimer's or dementia wing for those of us who become fully incapable.

While you remain able, you can live in your own patio home or apartment and keep your vehicle for your daily activities outside of the community. As your health declines or it becomes preferable to give up driving yourself, most facilities have a driver available to take you to shopping, medical appointments or bridge. These are in essence a self-contained community with health care available to you as needed. If you are married and your health declines, your spouse can keep their freedom while you are cared for medically.

With financial success comes freedom. If you have followed good financial planning advice and created a rainy day fund, what better place to use it than for a comfortable retirement existence?

There are continuing care facilities which require an equity buy-in with monthly fees, and those that are set up for strictly month to month occupancy. Many of our clients have expressed surprise at the monthly fees required for a care community existence. When you add up the costs to live outside the retirement facility you will find there is little difference. In addition, at this writing about 40% of the costs for care are considered a tax deduction for medical expenses.

Use the rainy day fund and take advantage of your good planning to allow you the freedom to live comfortably and without concern in your golden years.

# 32

## YO' MAMA AIN'T GOT NO MONEY

### AUGUST 2008

On occasion, I will meet people in my office who are seeking to hire a financial advisor. During the course of the interview, I will make a comment about the lack of savings they are committed to putting away.

Their response of "my dad has a lot of money and is very old so I will inherit a substantial sum one day and therefore need not concern myself with the details of saving money" is not as surprising to me today as it was the first few times I heard it.

It is acceptable to believe in a lot of things when living in the real world. You can believe in a higher being, that your cat understands what you are saying, divine intervention, low calorie chocolate, or even that the weather forecast for tomorrow is accurate.

But, if you believe and plan your financial future around your pending inheritance, then you should reconsider.

Here is a fact. The average life expectancy is 82 for a man of 65 today and 85 for a female. On a fixed income, a 20-year set of living expenses would triple with inflation averaging between 5 percent and 6 percent. Seeing a $3,000 monthly fixed expense rise to $9,000 could strain even a large nest egg.

Since most people tend to live within their means during retirement, the pressure on the nest egg is not normally felt in the early years of retirement. But, absent good planning by the retiree, when the pressures start to mount, the only course of action is often to spend the savings account (i.e., the children's inheritance).

Many retired parents are already helping an immediate family member. Some are helping their adult children buy a home they could not afford on their own. Grandparents are helping pay college costs for grandchildren (college tuition costs are rising much faster than recent inflation rates and faster than the 5 to 6 percent inflation rate suggested above).

More parents are divorced and are divorcing at older ages. As you would expect, supporting two households on one set of pensions and savings accounts is almost twice as expensive as supporting one household.

Have you heard the radio advertisements lately for a reverse mortgage? The target market for these loans is your retired mom and/or dad. Want to guess who will inherit the house if a reverse mortgage is in place on a dwelling? When a retiree speaks to us about this type of financial decision, they are not planning to inform their children they have taken this course of action.

Do you have a "ne'er do well" sibling? What are the odds mom or dad is helping them out with your inheritance? Many studies and financial articles report that the transfer of wealth from the older generation to the younger generation happens during the lifetime of the retiree (older generation for the purposes of this article).

Someone may be spending your inheritance and it may just be your mom, your dad, or your brother. Have you listened while a retiree talks about bailing someone out of a financial jam (credit card, student loan, vehicle payment) and thought how lucky they were?

That is someone's inheritance. I hope it was not the one you were planning on using to fund your retirement.

# 33

---

## FINANCIAL PLANNING POINTERS

### SEPTEMBER 1991

This column includes a listing of several techniques and ideas that have proven successful over the ten years I have been a financial advisor. You will notice that there are not any "quick" or "easy" solutions to attaining financial success. These financial planning ideas, however, have met the test of time. They include:

- Save a fixed percentage of your income on a regular schedule. The amount is not as important as the percentage. And, the percentage is less important than having a periodic form of savings.

- Spend more energy trying to increase your amount of savings than trying to increase the earnings on your savings. The rate you save will generate a greater return for you than the rate of earnings on your savings.

- Invest in assets you understand. Putting your money in things that confuse you often leads to dissatisfaction. It is generally safer to buy investments that are simple and easily understood than to buy assets that are more complex and bewildering.

- Have patience. If you have chosen quality investments with a good long-term track record, be patient. Allow them time to work for you and do not try to outsmart the investment markets.

- Do not spend saved money. The hardest goal to accomplish is to accumulate a sizeable savings account. Do not use these funds for consumer purchases. Make non-investment purchases from salary and cash flow. Use your savings to make investments.

- Diversify among several investment categories. Some people are reluctant to take a risk; others are reluctant to take a loss. By positioning your investments within several categories, you can minimize most of the risk involved in either case.

- Match your type of investment with your time horizon. Buy quality investments with proven track records and do not over-manage them. If you allow the investments to work for you, you will be less likely to make the common mistake of buying high and selling low. Often, doing less results in more.

- Buy your dwelling. If you plan to live in an area for four or more years, purchase your residence. The tax advantage combined with the potential for real estate appreciation greatly exceeds the guarantee of a zero gain available from being a tenant.

- Have a goal. Better yet, have several goals. Without a target, it is almost impossible to know if you are aiming in the right direction.

- Ask questions. Planning is an individual responsibility. Learn as much as you can. Knowledge will allow you to make better decisions independent of outside influence.

These techniques have helped many people become prosperous. So, while taking advantage of the strategies on this list is no guarantee of financial fortune, some combination will likely improve your chances of success.

# 34

---

## A FOOL AND HIS MONEY

### MAY 2006

*If you're serious about that little retirement account, here's how to hang on to it and watch it grow.*

If you know better, you do better (at least in theory). Here is a list of tips to help you protect your nest egg. You do not want to end up as the fool separated from his money.

1. Debt is bad. Avoid all debt. A home mortgage should be the limit to your indebtedness to others. NEVER borrow from your retirement plan.

2. Buy liability insurance. Sold in the form of an umbrella policy, this catastrophic liability protection covers a variety of accidents and the cost per year is quite low.

3. Do not buy the sizzle. Con artists masquerading as investment advisors, stockbrokers, or financial planners often offer a variety of past performance charts to suggest the future. They do not know what will happen in the future.

4. Do not buy out of fear. Insurance products and investment products with insurance wrappers are often sold to those fearful of the unknown.

5. Do not buy out of ignorance. If you do not understand how it works or what is involved in the purchase of the product, ask to have it explained to you again. If you still do not understand, walk away.

6. Have a durable power of attorney document. Name your spouse, adult child, or trusted friend to be in charge of your assets if you are unable to act on your own.

7. Check your credit report. You should know what others are reporting about you and the reports are available for free.

8. Diversify your investment account. No matter what your age, you should own some bonds, some international stocks, and some United States stocks in your investment portfolio.

9. While you are fully employed you should fully fund your personal retirement plan. Whether this is a company sponsored deferral account or an IRA, make the full annual contribution to the account.

10. Avoid the news shows that promote investment products, investment ideas and investment techniques. If these were really great "can't lose" ideas the investment advisor/broadcaster would put all of his money in the product and not tell you about it.

11. Ignore your friend's hot investment tip. It is not original (he heard it somewhere) and is likely to be inaccurate.

12. Wait a day or a week. Do not be impulsive. If someone is offering to sell you a financial product (insurance, investment, tax savings program), wait a day or more. If the idea still sounds like it has merit then consider owning it.

13. Keep it simple. If it sounds too good to be true or if it sounds too complicated, pass. The best ideas can be explained logically and simply.

You have worked hard for what you have, take some simple steps to keep and protect it. Do not be like the fool.

# 35

---

## SCAMS AND YOU

### SEPTEMBER 2016

As you have matured, so have the scammers. While you may still receive a call to fix your driveway since we "have some hot asphalt left on the truck" or an email that a Nigerian Prince wants you "to hold his million dollars in your bank account until he can get to America" chances are you already know about these tricks and will not be a victim.

However, there are new and more sophisticated forms of theft in play today. If you have a computer, you worry about "hackers" finding a way into your computer system and finding data they can use to steal something from you. Hackers find their way into a system through you. You let them into your computer by clicking on a link, replying to an email or failing to secure your internet connection. A hacker cannot easily get into your computer without you letting them in.

There are some rules to help you keep unauthorized people out of your computer system. These include knowing that the IRS, your Bank, your investment custodian, or your credit card company will never ask you for personal information including your driver's license, account passwords or social security number. They already have that information if they are legitimately who they say they are. Be on guard and suspicious of any email that requests your data. It is possible today for a scammer to create an email that appears to be legitimate. Any email that requires you to click on a link or an attachment should be viewed with a high level of skepticism. Microsoft is not going to call you to request access to your computer. Such a phone call is likely prelude to a scam by convincing you to provide access to your computer.

As you get older you are more likely to be a target of a scam. Make sure you have honest people assisting you with your personal affairs. Have a trusted advisor or family member you can call and ask a question before you make an irrevocable purchase of a large item or an unfamiliar investment. Many people make a purchase out of fear or greed that turns out to be a scam or a fabricated event. The old chestnut, "If it sounds too good to be true, then it probably is," still applies.

For many financial accounts you can have someone named as an interested party. By making a son or a daughter the interested party of your bank or brokerage account they can receive duplicate statements and see what happens inside the account. They cannot make trades or withdraw monies but they can monitor the account with you. Sometimes it is a good idea to have an extra set of eyes watching your assets. There are a lot of stories about people who have had monies moved out of their account and did not discover the fact until long after it was done.

Scammers are sophisticated enough to fool you into believing they are an injured friend or family member who needs your immediate financial action to rescue them from impending peril. We know of individuals who have been provoked into such action after receiving an email plea or even a phone call impersonating a loved one. Be highly suspicious of any request which suggests Western Union, PayPal, your credit card number or purchasing gift cards as remedy for such a rescue. You may be about to be scammed.

As you have matured, so have the scammers. Be aware and skeptical.

If you have made it this far, you are ahead of 79% of your peer group. Most people talk about making a better financial life for themselves and their family, but many take no action. You have done well reading about the changes you could make, now you need to make them.

As Dilbert said, "Change is good, you go first."

It is your turn to make improvements and we hope this book has given you the ideas to empower those changes.

# ABOUT THE AUTHOR

Andrew M. Hudick, MS, CFP (Andy) has provided integrated financial planning services to individuals and small businesses since founding Fee-Only Financial Planning, LC in 1981. His entrepreneurial spirit and endurance as a successful businessman gives him the unique perspective from which he still counsels. He earned the designation of Certified Financial Planner (CFP) in 1984 and is an SEC Registered Investment Advisor. He was one of the first individuals to be awarded the Master of Science degree in retirement planning from the College for Financial Planning in 1991. Andy served as National President of The National Association of Personal Financial Advisors (NAPFA) in 1995 where he was a member for over 25 years. Andy has been included in several financial planning books over the years quoting his experiences and also edited a booklet for NAPFA on how to build a fee-only financial planning practice. He has been selected to many top advisor lists including Worth Magazines Top 60 advisors in 1994 and their best advisor list in 1996, 1997, and 1998. In 2001 and 2002 Mutual Funds magazine chose him as one of the "100 Great Financial Planners from Coast to Coast" and he was chosen as one of the top 120 financial advisors for physicians in 1998 by Medical Economics.